HEART
OF THE
ENNEAGRAM

A COMPANION FOR DEEPENING
PERSONAL AND SPIRITUAL GROWTH

ISBN 978-1618460547

Produced and Distributed By:

Library Partners Press
ZSR Library
Wake Forest University
1834 Wake Forest Road
Winston-Salem, North Carolina 27106

 library partners press

a digital publishing imprint

www.librarypartnerspress.org

Manufactured in the United States of America

CONTENTS

INTRODUCTION

Welcome to *Heart of the Enneagram*. As students and teachers of the Enneagram for collectively more than 40 years, we are excited to offer this resource for those who are seeking to take a deeper dive into the tradition. The Enneagram is a system that offers clarity about self, compassion for others, and insight into relationships. Learning the Enneagram wakes us up to the habits and patterns of our lives, helping us recognize that we have the power to choose different ways to interact, respond, and engage with ourselves and others. In short, the Enneagram is a tool for bringing about more compassion and freedom in the world.

As we have encountered Enneagram teachings over the years, we have found that many of them tend to treat the Enneagram in a superficial way. Without venturing into the depths of this work, people can fall into the trap of using the Enneagram as one more way to reinforce, and even justify, our unhealthy habits and patterns. By contrast, our commitment is to go straight to the heart of the teaching in order to highlight the Enneagram's power to transform these habits and patterns.

We have learned from experience that simply knowing our Enneagram type and the types of those with whom we are in relationship only takes us so far. Knowledge and awareness are important first steps in the process of growth; however, true transformation comes only as we allow this knowledge and awareness to lead us to practices. These practices - new ways of engaging, perceiving, interacting - allow us to break the habitual patterns of our thoughts and behaviors and actually begin to rewire our brains. Engaging the Enneagram in this way means we take greater responsibility for our lives and subsequently experience deeper freedom.

Because of our desire to share this deeper freedom—a freedom that both of us have known and continue to experience through this particular way of exploring the Enneagram—we created *Heart of the Enneagram*. Starting with a podcast that explores each of the nine types through personal narratives of those who have discovered the power of this tool, we decided to create a companion book to support a deeper engagement with the Enneagram. This book offers practices, particularly in the form of journaling, that encourage the reader to reflect on quotes, questions, and statements that can help cultivate the inner observer and interrupt habitual thinking. While intended as a companion for the *Heart of the Enneagram* podcast, this book may also be used as a stand-alone resource for personal and spiritual growth.

Following the structure of the podcast, this book is divided into two sections—*Habits and Patterns of the Nine Types* and *Spiritual Dimensions of the Nine Types*. The first section contains basic information about each type—the focus of attention, vice, habit of mind, and reactivity of the type—followed by questions that help the reader take a deeper dive into that type. Section two explores the spiritual dimensions of the types by offering the virtue and enlightened spiritual perspective, questions for growth, and a prayer for each type. The book ends with a selection of resources including diagrams for motivation, focus of attention, vice, habit of mind, virtue, enlightened spiritual perspective, and heart names for each of the types.

The order of the types in this book and in the podcast might be curious to our readers, given that they are not in traditional numerical order. We intentionally chose to organize the types by the three triads, or centers of intelligence: heart (2,3,4), head (5,6,7), and body (8,9,1). Within the centers, we chose to begin with the central type of that triad as exemplified in the inner triangle of the Enneagram symbol. These types, 3, 6, 9, best illustrate the core of each of the centers so we present them first, followed by their triad companions. We hope that this is an effective way to learn more about the types as well as the centers of intelligence.

As you work through the questions throughout the book, we encourage you to reflect on those aspects of yourself that are reflections of each of the types. Even though you lead with one type, the questions for other types can be a helpful resource for understanding the little 1, 2, 3, 4, 5, 6, 7, 8, and 9 within each of us.

The *Heart of the Enneagram* podcast and companion book are intended for those who already have some familiarity with the Enneagram and their type. If you need more of an introduction to the Enneagram and a way to discover the primary type with which you lead, we encourage you to check out the "For Further Exploration" page at the end of the book.

If you find this podcast and companion book helpful in your personal and spiritual growth, please share that experience with others and encourage them to visit HeartoftheEnneagram. com, where they can subscribe to the podcast and purchase a copy of the book.

We dedicate this book to our many teachers and students over the years who have taught us the power and gift of the Enneagram, in particular Helen Palmer and David Daniels. We offer deep gratitude to Kaitlin Mundy who created the layout of this book, Toby Becker who designed the logo and book cover, Bernie Newton who offered his editing expertise, and Bill Kane of Library Partners Press who brought this vision to printed reality.

As you listen, read, and reflect on the power of the Enneagram through the *Heart of the Enneagram* podcast and this book, we invite you to look courageously and lovingly at what is.

Sandra C. Smith & Christopher T. Copeland
February 2018
HeartoftheEnneagram.com

HABITS & PATTERNS
OF THE NINE TYPES

3

TYPE THREE

"He asked, 'What do you feel called to?' and I said, 'To be a wind in other people's sails.' He then said, 'What's beautiful about that is, you can't pin a medal on the wind.'"

- Drew Jones, Director, Climate Interactive, Asheville, NC

GIFTS

- Competent
- Inspiring
- Positive, upbeat energy
- Motivated
- Engages easily with others
- Optimistic, yet realistic

FOCUS OF ATTENTION

Threes focus on putting forth an impressive image through successful performance. Driving questions for this type are: "What do I do next? What task needs completing? How might I be recognized by doing this project/task?" Doing, and then more doing, is the day's focus. Threes feel vulnerable when doing is absent.

VICE

The vice of deception has Threes believing that they are what they do. Their beingness is neglected and emotions are pushed aside for the sake of an impressive performance.

HABIT OF MIND

A winner/loser mental framework creates life as a competition. Vanity shows up as Threes ask, "What do you think of me? How am I doing?" Impressing with accomplishments takes center stage for Threes.

REACTIVITY

Fear of failure — of being unable to accomplish or perform — can bring forth reactivity. Additionally, when doing is blocked with slow processes and with indecisive people, Threes can react with impatience.

> *To do what is required of us in a situation without it becoming a role we identify with, is an essential lesson. We become most powerful if the action is performed for its own sake rather than as a means to protect or enhance our identity. We are most powerful when we are completely ourselves.*

> -Eckhart Tolle

OPENING THE HEART

How does a focus on task completion and accomplishment impact your life?

How important is recognition to you? How do you respond when you expect it and don't receive it?

In what ways do you craft an image of yourself? Who are you without a role?

How are you different than your efficiency?

When you are not the focus of your beloved's attention, what is that like for you? What supports you in staying with yourself?

INSIGHTS

As you read the quotes from Drew Jones and Eckhart Tolle and listen to the episode of *Heart of the Enneagram* about type Three, what strikes you, resonates with you, or raises questions for you? Name three insights that are becoming clearer to you.

The recognition, connection, and love I desire from others is found in unimpressive acts, in non-doing, and in offering my doubting, vulnerable self.

TYPE TWO

*Learning how to receive from others when you are in need,
and to allow that part of you to be seen,
has been so huge for me in my life.*

-Anna Kirby, Licensed Clinical Social Worker,
Duke University Medical Center, Durham, NC

GIFTS

- Positive spirit
- Enthusiastic
- Friendly
- Sensitive to others
- Good at assessing others
- Strong networking skills

FOCUS OF ATTENTION

Others' needs are front and center. Twos notice the likes and dislikes and the strengths of those important to them. Their focus is external and they move toward others for approval.

VICE

The vice of pride has Twos believing that they have no needs. Self-inflation occurs in the dual beliefs of "I can help you" and "I can do this and don't need help." The drive to be the "nice one" represses Two's own needs.

HABIT OF MIND

Am I approved or rejected? Do I want this person's approval? Flattery is a form of woo-ing others, almost in a seductive way. Twos see the world as highly relational, full of others in need. Needs are "out there" rather than residing in self.

REACTIVITY

Reactivity occurs when help goes unappreciated. The core fear for Twos is being dispensable, utterly useless, or rejected.

> *Because you believe in yourself,*
> *there is no need to convince others.*
> *Because you are content with yourself,*
> *you don't need others' approval.*
> *Because you accept yourself,*
> *the whole world accepts you.*

-Tao Te Ching

How does a focus on others' needs shape your life?

What is your own brand of approval-seeking, and what prompts this in you?

How do you use helping to control? How might receiving enable you to love more fully?

In what two areas do you most expect your beloved to know your needs?

In what ways are you willing and able to receive?

INSIGHTS

As you read the quotes from Anna Kirby and the Tao Te Ching, and listen to the episode of *Heart of the Enneagram* about type Two, what strikes you, resonates with you, or raises questions for you? Name three insights that are becoming clearer to you.

I am worthy and loved apart from the help I give.

TYPE FOUR

Gifts

- Creative
- Emotional intuition
- Emotional depth
- Thinks outside the box
- Eye for the beautiful
- Deals well with "quirky, out of the ordinary"

Focus of Attention

What is missing in a given situation or relationship keeps Fours feeling disappointed; therefore, their energy goes into seeking, searching, and longing. What is missing arises from the comparing mind: Fours compare reality to an introjected ideal and reality never measures up.

Vice

Envy — believing the grass is greener elsewhere — keeps longing in play and gratitude at a distance. This vice blinds Fours to all that is present and good. The feeling that they are either "too much" or "not enough" is a constant inner battle for Fours, and a way of abandoning the self. Self-rejection follows on the heels of envy.

Habit of Mind

A longing mind creates melancholy and supports the Four belief that the world is an abandoning place. Thoughts shift between "I'm superior" and "I'm inferior". How do I feel about this? What is the emotional tone? Is there enough emotional depth for me? Longing can feel juicier than attaining.

Reactivity

Fours react from a fear of being ordinary, being seen as one of the crowd or deficient in some way. This creates a drive to be unique or different. Addicted to peak experiences, Fours seek the highs and lows of life, which bring forth emotional intensity and give a sense of the extraordinary.

> *When our gratitude for the past is only partial, our hope for the future can never be full. As long as we remain resentful about. . . relationships that we wished had turned out differently, mistakes we wish we had not made, part of our heart remains isolated, unable to bear fruit in the new life ahead of us.*

-Henri Nouwen

Opening the Heart

The focus of attention of Type Four is on what is missing. How does this show up in your life?

The vice of Type Four is envy, meaning the grass is greener elsewhere. When do you experience this? How do you work with this?

In what ways do you abandon yourself? What helps you return to yourself?

How might the longing you experience for something outside yourself actually be a longing for yourself?

INSIGHTS

As you read the quotes from Jean Sexton and Henri Nouwen and listen to the episode of *Heart of the Enneagram* about type Four, what strikes you, resonates with you, or raises questions for you? Name three insights that are becoming clearer to you.

All I seek and long for is within me. I am all I want to be.

6

TYPE SIX

"Instead of resisting the phenomenon of uncertainty in the world, I am beginning to accept uncertainty. My experience of anxiety and fear in my life is directly related to my resisting uncertainty."

- Mirais Holden, Attorney, New Orleans, LA

GIFTS

- Imaginative
- Quick-witted
- Loyal
- Gifted problem solvers
- Engaging
- Excellent troubleshooters

FOCUS OF ATTENTION

For Sixes, worst-case thinking drives energy into a hypervigilant scanning for harm. This scanning creates a feeling of safety for Sixes as it allows them to anticipate and prepare for what might come. They become hyper-observant.

VICE

The unpredictable creates fear, therefore, Sixes see the world as a dangerous place. Fear drives worst-case scenario thinking.

HABIT OF MIND

A doubting mind creates hesitation. Am I safe? Can this authority be trusted? What might go wrong? Sixes troubleshoot, anticipate, and over-prepare as a way of creating a sense of certainty, a certainty they may substitute for trust.

REACTIVITY

Reactivity emanates from a fear of being alone or helpless and unable to cope with situations in a world perceived as unsafe. Also, reactivity occurs when being controlled or boxed in, which creates an unsafe feeling.

> *The desire for safety stands against every great and noble enterprise. If uncertainty is unacceptable to you, it turns into fear. If it is perfectly acceptable to you, it turns into complete aliveness, alertness, and creativity.*
>
> -Roman Philosopher Tacitus

The focus of attention of type Six is worst-case scenario thinking. How does this show up in your life?

The vice of type Six is fear, particularly as it relates to uncertainty and unpredictability. What is this fear like for you?

How does doubting get in the way loving fully? How are you different than your doubting?

How do you substitute certainty for trust?

When have you replaced authentic loving with security?

INSIGHTS

As you read the quotes from Mirais Holden and Tacitus and listen to the episode of *Heart of the Enneagram* about the Six, what strikes you, resonates with you, or raises questions for you? Name three insights that are becoming clearer to you.

All I need to feel secure is within me.

5
TYPE FIVE

I spend a lot of time in my head experiencing situations before I live through them. This is exhausting. In a way I'm using the very energy I'm trying to protect by trying to prepare and plan ahead for something you really can't plan ahead for.

- Brian Hayes, Master of Counseling Student, UNCG, Greensboro, NC **25**

GIFTS

- Thoughtful
- Curious
- Detail-oriented
- Thorough in research
- Desire to learn
- Pragmatic

FOCUS OF ATTENTION

Sensitive to intrusions, Fives detach to observe and analyze who or what may be too demanding. "What do I need to maintain my independence and privacy?" A focus on observing and detaching maximizes the inner world and diminishes the external.

VICE

Avarice is a withholding and rationing of energy and resources, which maintains the five's privacy and self-reliance. The core fear of being depleted keeps avarice in play.

HABIT OF MIND

Compartmentalized thinking separates thinking from feeling and helps to maintain privacy and secrecy. The rationing mind considers, "Do I have enough time and energy?" Fives believe that the world is too demanding and lacks generosity. This mentality of scarcity creates a stinginess in thinking and behaving.

REACTIVITY

Reactivity arises when intrusions or surprises demand a response. Additionally, being seen as incompetent drives reactivity.

> *I believe I will never quite know.*
> *Though I play at the edges of knowing,*
> *truly I know our part is not knowing,*
> *but looking, and touching, and loving, which is the way I walked on, softly,*
> *through the pale-pink morning light.*

26

- Mary Oliver

Opening the Heart

What does detachment, the focus of attention for Five, look like for you and what circumstances cause this to arise in you?

With whom do you play it safe with your heart? What does this cost you?

When has engaging offered you energy and nourishment?

When do you find yourself withholding information, energy, or time? What are you trying to protect?

When has the need for information or for privacy been a barrier to your loving fully?

How do you substitute knowledge for emotion?

INSIGHTS

As you read the quotes from Brian Hayes and Mary Oliver and listen to the episode of *Heart of the Enneagram* about type Five, what strikes you, resonates with you, or raises questions for you? Name three insights that are becoming clearer to you.

Abundance is within me.
When I give, the world returns the giving.

7

TYPE SEVEN

To be empty sounds negative, but it really isn't. I should embrace it as if that's my time to slow down, that quiet time I need.

-Vicki Banks, Vice President of Human Resources,
Biltmore Company, Asheville, NC

Gifts

- Quick Mind
- Curious
- Playful
- Imaginative
- Visionary
- Integrating and synthesizing ideas

Focus of Attention

Best-case thinking and fun possibilities move the conversation or the process along to the "next." Seeking stimulation keeps the energy up, which causes the Seven to feel positive and free.

Vice

Sevens experience gluttony, a desire to taste a little of everything. Not wanting to miss out, they are attracted to the new—new ideas, projects, adventures, and people. Filling up on one, they move to the next. Tasting without "digesting" the whole experience is common among Sevens.

Habit of Mind

Sevens have a planning mind that synthesizes ideas and concepts and considers future possibilities. In this planning mind, questions arise such as "Is this fun or can it be fun?" and "Do I feel free or do I feel limited?"

Reactivity

Fear of being trapped, limited, or missing something brings up reactivity in Sevens; therefore, slow processing, confining rules, and emotional pain may be avoided.

The end of our exploring will be to arrive where we started and know that place for the first time.

-T.S. Eliot

OPENING THE HEART

How does best-case possibility, the focus of attention for type Seven, show how up in your life?

What are other-imposed limitations like for you? How do you work with them?

When does reframing or deflecting difficult news show up most in your life?

Why is emptiness scary for you?

INSIGHTS

As you read the quotes from Vicki Banks and T.S. Eliot and listen to the episode of *Heart of the Enneagram* about type Seven, what strikes you, resonates with you, or raises questions for you? Name three insights that are becoming clearer to you.

Boundaries and limitations offer a gentle framework
that allows me to feel fulfilled and complete.

9

TYPE NINE

The watch words I've developed for myself with insights I've gained from the Enneagram are to wake up, discern, and act.

-Joy McIver, Attorney, Asheville, NC

GIFTS

- Tolerant
- Steady & calm
- Can see big picture
- Good listener when present
- Seeks fairness
- Ability to see numerous viewpoints

FOCUS OF ATTENTION

Others' agendas replace the Nine's agenda, which can lead to accommodation and acquiescence. Nines' priorities and wants become expendable as they self-erase to avoid conflict and stay in their comfort zone. They distract themselves from important priorities with a focus on nonessentials. For Nines, anger can feel too big to express, so they numb out to feelings as well as to their own agenda.

VICE

Slothfulness is a laziness toward the self. In everyday life, it looks like forgetting one's priorities or not expressing an opinion when it may differ from others' opinions. This vice hides Nines in a numbed-out routine that feels lackluster. Nines can feel that they are living a discounted version of themselves.

HABIT OF MIND

Merging with others' agendas and "going along to get along" is an easy path, but one that is life-denying for Nines. The Nine mind can seem foggy and unclear, which leads to self-erasing. To Nines, the world is ignoring them, so why not join in. However, at some point, anger stirs and serves to wake up Nines to their own desires and priorities.

REACTIVITY

Feeling that they are unacknowledged or insignificant creates a reactive posture for Nines. Not feeling seen or heard is almost an expectation for Nines and can be a self-fulfilling prophecy when Nines hide themselves.

> *The breezes at dawn have secrets to tell you. Don't go back to sleep.*
> *You must ask for what you really want.*
> *Don't go back to sleep.*
> *People are going back and forth*
> *Across the doors where the two worlds touch. The door is round and open.*
> *Don't go back to sleep.*

34

-Rumi

OPENING THE HEART

The focus of attention of type Nine is on others' agendas. How does this show up in your life?

When you are avoiding conflict, what do you do?

The vice of type Nine is self-forgetting. What tells you that this is in play?

In what ways do you remember yourself? What helps you return to you?

Remember times when you were seen and heard. How did you foster those experiences?

INSIGHTS

As you read the quotes from Joy McIver and Rumi and listen to the episode of *Heart of the Enneagram* about type Nine, what strikes you, resonates with you, or raises questions for you? Name three insights that are becoming clearer to you.

Peace isn't an absence of conflict but an ability to hold polarities, which honors the both/and of your agenda and my agenda.

TYPE EIGHT

Trust is incredibly hard. I rarely trust people unless I've seen their vulnerability first. That is my default setting.

- Brian Ammons, Chaplain and Director of Spiritual Life,
Warren Wilson College, Swannanoa, NC

GIFTS

- Direct & Clear
- Generous
- Willing to initiate
- Hardworking
- Loyal
- Dependable
- Energetic

FOCUS OF ATTENTION

The focus on control brings forth questions like "Who has power and are they fair?" and "What needs my directing?" With easy access to life force energy, Eights activate quickly. Waiting is difficult and feels vulnerable.

VICE

Lust is an instinctual drive to have something now, to have the desire satisfied immediately. It isn't necessarily sexual. The sights of the eight narrow on what is desired.

HABIT OF MIND

Eights see the world as dualistic. An all-or-nothing, now-or-never mental framework creates black and white thinking: "Are you with me or against me?" Eights can test for powerful/powerless postures. They may hold an unconscious belief that the world is unfair and against them.

REACTIVITY

Fear of being unjustly controlled or feeling powerless can activate a show of strength. Eights may push back against "silly rules" or anyone who tries to control them and what matters to them.

> *When you make the truth too definite you make it too small.*

-Samuel Taylor Coleridge

Opening the Heart

The focus of attention of type Eight is taking control. How does this show up in your life?

The vice of type Eight is lust or excess. How do you know when you are using too much energy to have a desire satisfied?

When does certainty get activated most strongly for you?

When you need support or need to be taken care of, how do you express this?

Why is waiting so scary for you? What helps you wait?

INSIGHTS

As you read the quotes from Brian Ammons and Samuel Taylor Coleridge and listen to the episode of *Heart of the Enneagram* about type Eight, what strikes you, resonates with you, or raises questions for you? Name three insights that are becoming clearer to you.

I can claim the power that resides in the tenderness of my heart.

TYPE ONE

"The challenge for me will always be to try to see the good thing or the thing I can celebrate in a situation before I automatically go to, 'Well that's wrong,' whatever it is.

-Joyce Hollyday, Author, Asheville, NC

Gifts

- Diplomatic
- Strong work ethic
- Fair
- Orderly
- Organized
- Reforming

Focus of Attention

Ones scan the environment to see what is wrong—what needs improving or correcting. Creating order in a world that seems chaotic is part of the daily task as Ones work toward improving the world, being responsible and good.

Vice

Anger arises at what isn't right with the world, which fuels the judging mind and a righteous indignation. Ones rarely relate to anger as their vice since it isn't "right" to be angry, so it is often expressed as impatience or resentment. Self-deprivation, denying their wants, often gives rise to anger.

Habit of Mind

Right or wrong, ordered or disordered, fair or unfair, these are the categories of thinking for Ones. "The world is chaotic and I can improve it." "What is the responsible thing to do now?" An inner critique of self or other (or both) tends to be constant.

Reactivity

Fear of being wrong, bad, or inappropriate creates reactivity for Ones. Mistakes feel like death, so Ones strive toward what is right.

You don't have to be good. You do not have to walk on your knees for a hundred miles through the desert repenting. You only have to let the soft animal of your body love what it loves.

-Mary Oliver

The focus of attention of type One is on what needs improving or correcting. How does "fixing" or "being right" show up in your life?

The vice of type One is anger or resentment, which usually arises when Ones push aside their own desires in order to be responsible. When do you engage the "ought tos" rather than your "want tos?"

When is play and relaxing most acceptable to you? Least acceptable?

Who are you aside from one who improves?

INSIGHTS

As you read the quotes from Joyce Hollyday and Mary Oliver and listen to the episode of *Heart of the Enneagram* about type One, what strikes you, resonates with you, or raises questions for you? Name three insights that are becoming clearer to you.

Allowing the instinctual, spontaneous energy to arise creates
a suppleness that appreciates difference and blesses the unblessed self.

SPIRITUAL DIMENSIONS
OF THE NINE TYPES

THE AUTHENTIC HEART

3

TYPE THREE

It's really only in the place of not doing that I can begin to connect with my true inner self.

-Gerry Fathauer, Aura Intuitive & Certified Narrative Enneagram Teacher, Cleveland, OH

Virtue

Honesty allows Threes to fully understand that their performance isn't who they are. Through honesty, the genuine self emerges, complete with emotions and a heart that offers authentic connection.

Enlightened Spiritual Perspective

Holy Hope brings the recognition that the Three isn't responsible for all of the doing. From this place, Threes understand they are a part of humanity, not a separate "doing good." We are in this together!

> *The Master leads by emptying people's minds and filling their cores, by weakening their ambition and toughening their resolve. S/he helps people lose everything they know, everything they desire, and creates confusion in those who think they know. Practice non-doing and everything will fall into place.*
>
> -Tao Te Ching

When you read this quote from the Tao Te Ching, what resonates most with the Three within you?

THE AUTHENTIC HEART

What does honesty mean to you? Where does it show up most in your life?

Who are you when you are honest with yourself? In other words, who are you in your own eyes?

How might your fear be a gateway to loving more fully?

When have you experienced authenticity in your relationships and how do you know this?

INSIGHTS

As you read and listen to the words of Gerry Fathauer in this episode of *Heart of the Enneagram* about the spiritual dimensions of type Three, what strikes you, resonates with you, or raises questions for you? Name three insights that are becoming clearer to you.

PRAYER FOR THE THREE

Divine Love,

I thank you for the motivation and energy to work hard and succeed as well as for the ease with which I can engage and inspire others. Resting in your boundless love, help me to trust that I am more than my doing and greater than the images I create. I long to be my deepest, truest self, but I sometimes fear that if I strip away the masks I will not find anyone there. Give me the courage to lay aside my constant doing so that I may receive the gift of your infinite love for me, which is not dependent on my accomplishments. Help me to know that underneath the roles I inhabit, at the core of my being, I am loved simply for who I am.

Non-doing supports my Being, which is impressive enough.

THE RECEPTIVE HEART

2

TYPE TWO

What if my giving is not appreciated or received or reciprocated? Am I still happy giving? That's a clean giving.

-Mary Beth Gwynn, Soul Awareness Guide, Asheville, NC

VIRTUE

Humility brings forth a balance for type Two as pride recedes. The "yes" is balanced with the "no," and there is a natural flow of giving and receiving.

ENLIGHTENED SPIRITUAL PERSPECTIVE

Holy Freedom is experienced when Twos are free from their own need to be needed and no longer fear disappointing others. Here, Twos are aware of their own needs, ask for support, and receive naturally.

> *There is a force within that gives you life-*
> *Seek that.*
> *In your body there lies a priceless jewel-*
> *Seek that.*
> *If you are in search of your greatest treasure*
> *Don't look outside.*
> *Look within and seek that.*

-Rumi

When you read this quote from Rumi, what resonates most with the Two within you?

THE RECEPTIVE HEART

When has receiving enabled you to love more fully?

What enables you to ask for help or support?

Who are you when you are free from others' approval and expectations?

Insights

As you read and listen to the words of Mary Beth Gwynn in the episode of *Heart of the Enneagram* about the spiritual dimensions of type Two, what strikes you, resonates with you, or raises questions for you? Name three insights that are becoming clearer to you.

Prayer for the Two

Loving Lap,

As I rest in your care, anchor me in my humility that I may know myself more fully, honoring my limitations as well as my gifts. I desire to be real. I desire to be discerning in what is mine to do and not to do. Empty me of my need for approval and my lists of all who need me. Guide me in the ways of being receptive, that I may participate more fully in my own life, offering myself compassion as well as others. Dissolve my pride, Holy One, that I may be more available to my own needs, and to the present unfolding without agendas. Open my heart to the support of others. Remind me of my interdependence so that I no longer inflate my own abilities but am grounded in the reality of who I am. Grant me a willingness to be open to what arises, that I may find my freedom in your unconditional love.

A willingness to receive what is offered before me and to lean on another supports my process of self-acceptance.

THE GRATEFUL HEART

4

TYPE FOUR

"There is a sense of completeness, of fullness, as opposed to being overwhelmed. I look at the situation to see if I can respond with some kind of creative openness. In a way that would be equanimity for me. A lot of times it is enlivening for me.

-John Amen, Poet & Certified Narrative Enneagram Teacher,
Charlotte, NC

Virtue

Equanimity brings forth a mental and emotional evenness. Here, Fours experience a deep calm, and their presence deepens and the longing ceases. They know in their marrow that nothing is missing.

Enlightened Spiritual Perspective

Holy Origin is the place where Fours recognize that all are connected to Source. They are not abandoned but held in this connection, and seeking relaxes into gratefulness.

> *What We Need is Here*
> *Geese appear high over us,*
> *pass, and the sky closes. Abandon,*
> *as in love or sleep, holds*
> *them to their way, clear*
> *in the ancient faith: what we need*
> *is here. And we pray, not*
> *for new earth or heaven, but to be*
> *quiet in heart, and in eye,*
> *clear. What we need is here.*

-Wendell Berry

When you read this quote from Wendell Berry, what resonates most with the Four within you?

THE GRATEFUL HEART

What does equanimity mean to you? Where does it show up most in your life?

When do you feel most connected to Source? What allows this to occur?

How do you discover the miracle in the ordinary?

Insights

As you read and listen to the words of John Amen in the episode of *Heart of the Enneagram* about the spiritual dimensions of type Four, what strikes you, resonates with you, or raises questions for you? Name three insights that are becoming clearer to you.

Prayer for the Four

Weaver of Beauty,

Thank you for seeking me, for never stopping to seek me. Open me to the intimate connection between us that I may rest in your grace. Empty me of all the ways I abandon myself, these self-rejections that evoke shame. Soften my comparing mind that I may know gratitude for what I have and for who I am. Guide me in the path of appreciation for the beauty and possibility that surrounds me, that is within me. Sacred Source of my life, ground me in my inner calm and remind me of the holy and the beautiful in the ordinary. Open my eyes and my heart to see your grace-filled touch in all of life. From this "seeing" I know there really are no ordinary moments, for all is sacred.

Simple sadness and simple joy expand the heart,
allowing me to feel a deep calm as I connect with others.

THE COURAGEOUS HEART

6

TYPE SIX

Solid Ground is meaningful for me as an image of God. This gives me a sense of safety, a sense that I'm being held. Sometimes I've used the phrase 'Near One.' It reminds me that God is present, near me, and in me, and not out there somewhere.

-Debbi Horton, Spiritual Director & Certified Narrative Enneagram Teacher, St. Paul, MN

Virtue

The virtue of Six is courage, meaning the courage to look within and know there is a solid foundation, Essence, from which Sixes can draw strength. "You have you to count on" (David Daniels, MD).

Enlightened Spiritual Perspective

Faith arises when Sixes trust themselves. This is a faith in self that moves into faith in all, in the Holy, in the sacred unfolding of life. Faith doesn't need to know ahead of time.

> *Keep walking, though there's no place to get to.*
> *Don't try to see through the distances.*
> *That's not for human beings. Move within,*
> *But don't move the way fear makes you move.*

-Rumi

As you read this quote by Rumi, how do the words speak to the Six inside of you?

THE COURAGEOUS HEART

Name a person in your life that you consider courageous. What qualities does this person have that speak to you of courage?

At this point in your life, how do you experience and express courage? What circumstances prompt courage to arise in you?

Remember a time when faith emerged to strengthen your resolve or a decision. Describe yourself in this moment.

What supports you in growing your faith?

INSIGHTS

As you read and listen to the words of Debbi Horton in this episode of *Heart of the Enneagram* about the spiritual dimensions of type Six, what strikes you, resonates with you, or raises questions for you? Name three insights that are becoming clearer to you.

PRAYER FOR THE SIX

Sacred Ground of my Being,

You are within me and beyond me, forever present. Your love enfolds me as I go about my days. I am not alone. My suspicions fade when held in your unwavering assurance of me. Empty me now of my anxieties, doubts and imaginings. Assuage my fears. Create in me a refuge for trusting myself. Remind me that all I need is within me as I stand on my own solid foundation. Knowing your steady Ground is with me, I move forward in an uncertain world. Guide me as I travel the path of courage so I may lean into myself when the waters are troubled and have faith in the unfolding. Hold me in the fearful times, hold me in the fearless times. In your Holy Ground I rise to offer my full and powerful self in each moment.

My courageous heart holds me in uncertain times.

THE GENEROUS HEART

5
TYPE FIVE

There is a really large source of limitless energy out there, and I think I'm connected to it. Let's go!

-Lawrence Womack, Rector of St. Augustine's Episcopal Church, Brooklyn, NY

Virtue

Driven by the belief in "more than enough," non-attachment allows Fives to offer an open-handed response to life.

Enlightened Spiritual Perspective

Holy Omniscience is more than knowledge, it is wisdom. This wisdom is a full knowing when we engage with life, sharing ourselves and engaging in relationships with all three centers of intelligence accessible.

> *Someone spoke to me last night,*
> *told me the truth. Just a few words,*
> *but I recognized it.*
> *I knew I should make myself get up,*
> *write it down, but it was late,*
> *and I was exhausted from working*
> *all day in the garden, moving rocks.*
> *Now, I remember only the flavor—*
> *not like food, sweet or sharp.*
> *More like a fine powder, like dust.*
> *And I wasn't elated or frightened,*
> *but simply rapt, aware.*
> *That's how it is sometimes—*
> *God comes to your window,*
> *all bright light and black wings,*
> *and you're just too tired to open it.*

-Dorianne Laux

When you read this poem by Dorianne Laux, what resonates most with the Five within you?

The Generous Heart

What does non-attachment mean to you? When are you able to live this?

When do you engage the wisdom of the body and wisdom of the heart? What allows you to engage this wisdom?

When do you experience "more than enough?" (Abundance)

What are you afraid to ask for that you really want?

Insights

As you read and listen to the words of Lawrence Womack in the episode of *Heart of the Enneagram* about the spiritual dimensions of type Five, what strikes you, resonates with you, or raises questions for you? Name three insights that are becoming clearer to you.

Prayer for the Five

Abundant and Never-ending Source,

I give thanks for my thoughtful and curious mind as well as a continuing hunger for learning. Help me to engage more with others so that I may discover the gift of your overflowing energy and resources comes not simply from within, but from the world around me. Give me the courage to reach out more to people and to trust that by being present with others, I will receive far more life and energy than I can imagine. Grounded in your unending source, may I have the generosity to share my insights with those I meet, and the courage to offer them my heart.

Full wisdom arises when I'm grounded and my heart is generous.

7 THE QUIET HEART

TYPE SEVEN

"I see in my life where choosing things and sticking with them has brought depth and grounding and belonging and joy instead of scattered excitement."

-Molly Bolton, Medical Intensive Care Unit Chaplain, Cleveland, OH

Virtue

Constancy allows Sevens a focus that brings thoroughness and completion to projects, tasks, and relationships. It brings depth.

Enlightened Spiritual Perspective

Holy Work is the work of being present to what is arising in this moment. The tendency for Sevens is to move into the future to avoid possible limitations or emotional difficulties in the present. The fear of being limited leads Sevens to positively reframe their perception of what is.

> *The mystery does not get clearer by repeating the question,*
> *Nor is it bought going to amazing places.*
> *Until you have kept your eyes and your wanting still for fifty years,*
> *You don't begin to cross over from confusion.*

-Rumi

When you read this Rumi quote, what resonates most with the Seven within you?

THE QUIET HEART

What does constancy mean to you? Where does it show up most in your life?

How are you cultivating more capacity for presence, a presence that abides through boredom and sorrow?

Remember a time when another offered you a kind presence when you were hurting. What was it like to share your pain/hurt with another and have that deepen your relationship?

How might being present to your sadness allow you to love more fully?

INSIGHTS

As you read and listen to the words of Molly Bolton in the episode of *Heart of the Enneagram* about the spiritual dimensions of type Seven, what strikes you, resonates with you, or raises questions for you? Name three insights that are becoming clearer to you.

PRAYER FOR THE SEVEN

Holy Creativity,

Your love and grace know no limits. You offer the completion I seek. Gently guide me to my fulfillment, awaiting me when I rest in the calm of present moment. My mind seeks such calm. Empty me now of my obsessive planning and all the ideas that overwhelm me. Allow my energy to deepen me, not scatter me, so that I experience the gifts offered each moment, gifts that lead to my wholeness. Guide me to my heart, that I may feel not only my joy, but the richness of my sadness. Deep down, I recognize that it is my sadness that I seek, it is limitation I desire. For both bring me home to my deeper self where I find the freedom to be me. Guide me on the path toward reverence.

My complete presence makes space for both joy and sadness.

9

THE ALIVE HEART

TYPE NINE

Unlived life takes more energy than lived life.

-Guy Sayles, Retired Pastor and Assistant Professor of Religion
at Mars Hill University, Mars Hill, NC

VIRTUE

When practicing Right Action (action that supports self-remembering), Nines show up by being clear about their priorities and claiming what they want and need. This brings an ability to practice both/and: my agenda AND your agenda can both be heard and honored.

ENLIGHTENED SPIRITUAL PERSPECTIVE

Holy Love is the work of accepting and loving the self so fully that this love moves beyond the self to others. It requires a separate self, one that is honored and claimed. When Nines find themselves in Holy Love, they understand Divine Union.

Unconditional love is not so much about how we receive and endure each other as it is about the deep vow to never under any conditions stop bringing the flawed truth of who we are to each other.

-Mark Nepo

When you read this quote from Mark Nepo, what resonates most with the Nine within you?

THE ALIVE HEART

What does self-remembering mean to you? When does this occur in your life and what enables it to arise?

What do you most celebrate about yourself?

Remember a time when you felt passionately, when your heart was alive and your mind clear. Describe yourself in that moment, paying particular attention to your body sensations, including your voice.

How might befriending your anger be a gateway to your loving fully?

INSIGHTS

As you read and listen to the words of Guy Sales in the episode of *Heart of the Enneagram* about the spiritual dimensions of type Nine, what strikes you, resonates with you, or raises questions for you? Name three insights that are becoming clearer to you.

PRAYER FOR THE NINE

One Who Sees Me and Knows Me,

For my gentleness of spirit, openness of heart, and ability to remain steady and calm, I give you thanks. While I long to be seen and known by others, help me recognize that by going along to get along and not sharing my own opinions and desires, I reinforce my sense of invisibility. Give me the wisdom to recognize that by owning and offering my own deepest feelings, I will not lose my inner peace but will create an opportunity for true intimacy and connection with others. Grant me the grace to not forget myself, to choose to be fully alive, and to know beyond a doubt that I matter.

My great love—including love of myself—
makes a significant impact in the world.

8

THE TENDER HEART

TYPE EIGHT

Struggle means I've got to do something to make it harder. Can it be harder just on its own? Can it just be there on its own? Then I don't have to get up and make it harder every single minute of every single day.

- Amy Greene, Director of Spiritual Care, Cleveland Clinic, Cleveland, OH

Virtue

Innocence has no armor and is unguarded. For Eights, this means no opinions, no certainty, only an openness to what others offer and to what arises in the moment.

Enlightened Spiritual Perspective

Holy Truth is the truth of oneness. The world is non-dual, there is no "us" and "them;" we are all connected in unity.

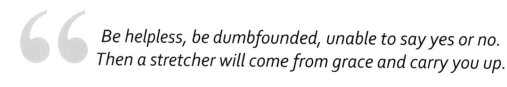

> *Be helpless, be dumbfounded, unable to say yes or no.*
> *Then a stretcher will come from grace and carry you up.*
>
> -Rumi

When you read this Rumi quote, what resonates most with the Eight within you?

The Tender Heart

What does innocence mean to you? When do you remember a time of no opinion? What was that like? Where do you find your power when you have no opinion?

How are you kind to yourself?

Remember a time when you stood in Holy Truth, in the Oneness of all. What did you learn from that moment? How might you cultivate more of these non-dual moments when the narrative of "you are with me or against me" arises?

How might your vulnerability be a gateway to your loving fully?

INSIGHTS

As you read and listen to the words of Amy Greene in the episode of *Heart of the Enneagram* about the spiritual dimensions of type Nine, what strikes you, resonates with you, or raises questions for you? Name three insights that are becoming clearer to you.

PRAYER FOR THE EIGHT

Loving Protector,

Watch my back as I wade into the waters of waiting and hold me as I delay my impact. Empty me of my need to assert myself or to blame others when life seems out of control. Soften the walls surrounding my heart, the rigid boundaries, my strong opinions. Embrace me as I wait, so that I may know the richness in stillness and open my heart to the affection of others. May I be present in each moment without judgment and without fear, knowing that you have my back. Ground me in your gentle and loving presence that I may be gentle and loving with myself and others. Remind me each day that we are all one and that in our unity we find hope, and in vulnerability we discover loving support.

Vulnerability, need, and a willingness to be touched offer a new kind of power and beauty that can emerge in the practice of waiting.

THE GRACE-FILLED HEART

1

TYPE ONE

"You ask how I experience this kind of acceptance or serenity, and it feels like a descent or an ascent. For me it feels like a sinking into a place where differences and distinctions dissolve; and, of course, with that, right and wrong go away for a little while."

-Michelle Voss Roberts, Dean for Academic Affairs & Associate Professor of Theology, Wake Forest University School of Divinity, Winston-Salem, NC

Virtue

Serenity comes when Ones move into acceptance of what is arising in each moment. No longer improving or fixing, Ones relax into peace and offer a non-judging presence.

Enlightened Spiritual Perspective

Holy Perfection is the deep understanding that all is inherently perfect as it is. Everyone, everything is as it "should" be. Categories of good and bad, perfect and imperfect recede.

Out beyond the ideas of wrongdoing and
Right doing, there is a field. I'll meet you there.
When the soul lies down in that grass,
the world is too full to talk about.
Ideas, language, even the phrase "each other"
no longer makes sense.

-Rumi

When you read this Rumi quote, what resonates most with the One within you?

THE GRACE-FILLED HEART

The virtue of your type is serenity. What does this mean to you? What circumstances allow this virtue to arise?

What allows you to name your task or project as good enough?

Remember a time when you knew that not one thing needed improving and you relaxed into this knowing. Describe yourself in that moment.

Ones can show they care by improving. What does caring beyond improving look like for you?

INSIGHTS

As you read and listen to the words of Michelle Voss Roberts in the episode of *Heart of the Enneagram* about the spiritual dimensions of type One, what strikes you, resonates with you, or raises questions for you? Name three insights that are becoming clearer to you.

PRAYER FOR THE ONE

Divine Grace,

For a willingness to work hard, a desire for ongoing improvement, and a passion for fairness, I give you thanks. Help me to choose the peace that comes with accepting things as they are, rather than always seeing them as I think they should be. Give me the courage to relax my judging mind, trusting that everything is inherently perfect as it is. Show me the path of play that I might release my tension and fall gently into the abundant grace of your loving embrace.

I find deep peace when I cease improving.

RESOURCES

Motivation

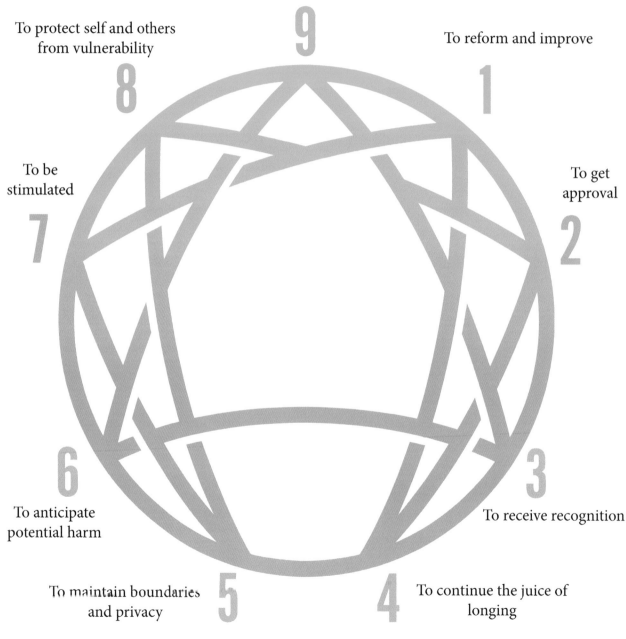

To keep the peace

To protect self and others
from vulnerability

To reform and improve

To be
stimulated

To get
approval

To anticipate
potential harm

To receive recognition

To maintain boundaries
and privacy

To continue the juice of
longing

Focus of Attention

Others' agendas

9

Seeing error

Taking control

8

1

Best-case thinking

7

Others' needs

2

Worst-case scenario

6

Tasks to do

3

Detaching & observing

5

Seeing what is missing

4

VICE / HABIT OF MIND

Slothfulness /
Indolence

Lust /
Blame

Anger /
Judgment

Gluttony /
Planning

Pride /
Flattery

Doubting /
Fear

Deception /
Vanity

Avarice /
Stinginess

Envy /
Melancholy

Virtue / Enlightened Spiritual Perspective

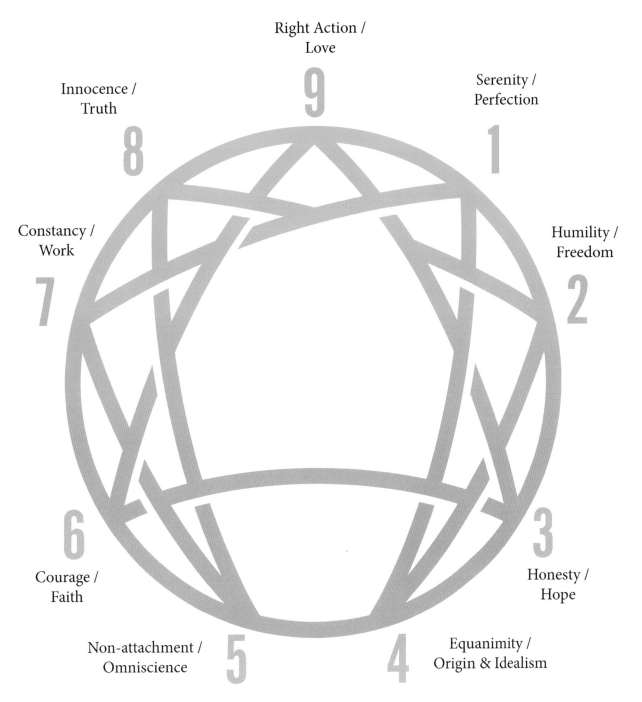

Right Action /
Love

Serenity /
Perfection

Innocence /
Truth

Humility /
Freedom

Constancy /
Work

Honesty /
Hope

Courage /
Faith

Equanimity /
Origin & Idealism

Non-attachment /
Omniscience

THE OPEN HEART

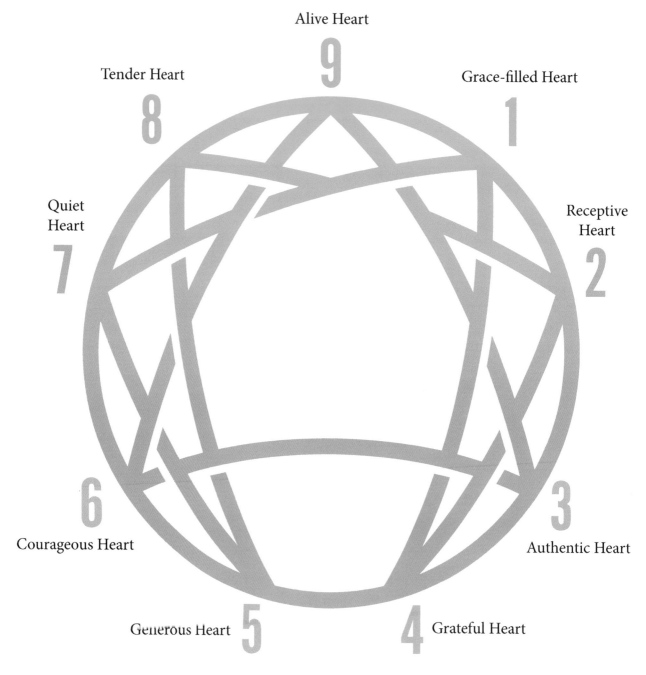

Alive Heart

Tender Heart

Grace-filled Heart

Quiet
Heart

Receptive
Heart

Courageous Heart

Authentic Heart

Generous Heart

Grateful Heart

For Further Exploration

Books

The Essential Enneagram, David Daniels, MD & Virginia Price

The Enneagram: Understanding Self and Others, Helen Palmer

The Enneagram in Love and Work, Helen Palmer

Facets of Unity: The Enneagram of Holy Ideas, A.H. Almaas

The Complete Enneagram, Beatrice Chestnut

The Enneagram of Passions and Virtues, Sandra Maitri

The Spiritual Dimensions of the Enneagram, Sandra Maitri

The Integral Enneagram, Susan Rhodes

Websites

HeartoftheEnneagram.com

AlchemyWorksEvents.com

NarrativeEnneagram.com

TheEnneagramAtWork.com

Printed in Great Britain
by Amazon

45585587R00053